Bottom Dog Press
Literature of the Midwest
c/o Firelands College/ Huron, OH 44839

STEAM DUMMY

&

FRAGMENTS FROM THE FIRE
The Triangle Shirtwaist Company
Fire of March 25, 1911

Poems

Chris Llewellyn

Midwest Writers Series
Bottom Dog Press
Huron, Ohio

Acknowledgements

STEAM DUMMY

The author wishes to thank the District of Columbia Arts and
Humanities Commission for a 1990 Artists Grant, the National
Endowment for the Arts for a 1988 Fellowship in Literature,
and the Ohio Arts Council and Eleanor Wilner for publication
support of this book.

Also thanks to these critical readers of the *Steam Dummy*
poems: Anne Becker, Maria Boza, Don Colburn, Judy Daniels,
Toi Derricotte, Tom Kirlin, Thomas Lux, Kenneth Rosen,
Grace Schulman, Larry Smith, and John Skoyles.

The author acknowledges the continuing support of the
Capitol Hill Poetry Group.

Special thanks is due to LeRoy Leibel and the employees of
Aristo Drycleaners.

*FRAGMENTS FROM THE FIRE: THE TRIANGLE
SHIRTWAIST COMPANY FIRE OF MARCH 25, 1911*
by Chris Llewellyn was the winner of the Walt Whitman
Award for 1986, sponsored by The Academy of American Poets.
Judge for 1986: Maxine Kumin.

This is a revised edition of that book which was originally
published by Viking Press in 1987.

Special thanks is due to the late Leon Stein, author of the only
book written exclusively on this tragic event.

The author also wishes to thank the District of Columbia Arts
and Humanities Commission for a 1984 grant which funded
technical assistance for the manuscript and to acknowledge the
continued support of the Capitol Hill Poetry Group, the Jennie
McKean Moore Writing Program, and the Festival of Poets and
Poetry at St. Mary's College of Maryland.

An audio tape of Chris Llewellyn reading from these
two books is available from Bottom Dog Press ($8.95).

**[A detailed listing of publication credits is presented at
the back of this volume.]**

*Funded Through
Ohio Arts Council*

CONTENTS

STEAM DUMMY

His Bones/My Bones

Facts Written on Water

The Sheaves

A Little Elevation

FRAGMENTS FROM THE FIRE

Fostoria, Ohio, *Jan 15* 193 *4*

Harry Dean

Sign painter

PORTER'S DRY CLEANING
AND DYE WORKS

ESTABLISHED IN 1889
PHONE 34

HENRY L. PORTER & SON, PROPS.
115 PERRY ST.

All Bills Must Be Settled 1st of Each Month

774

1/11	hat D C B		$ .50
2/2	bathrobe D C P	104	.75
2/2	pants D C P	1152	.40
2/22	suit D C P		75
		$	2.40

Pd in full
2/12/34

1844

3/23	l'coat D C P	.75

Pd 5/19/34

STEAM DUMMY

HIS BONES/MY BONES

Dedicated to the memory of my father
William Thomas Porter (1906-1957)

IN SOUTH DAKOTA, MY OHIO MEMORY

In Wounded Knee the rainfall swells
the red clay, retelling bloody murders.

When long ago Yellow Hair, Long Knives
did their slaughter, down sunrise,

earth-under, Great Grandfather worked
in mines. From a lantern hat

on his coal black hair, a canary
flame lit his bones/my bones.

FROM A CHIPPED CUP

The Hopi say wherever there is mist
the gods are present: in fog
shrouded corn fields, in iron
kettle steam, in mesquite smoke
that hangs like a scrim.

But here in the prairie town
of northwest Ohio, naphtha
steam shoots from the blowhole.

An exhaust pipe points across
the alley, points at our house
for three generations.

A gray condensation has pitted
the timbers, and sickly mist settles
in doorways and windows.

There Mother's sweet potato vine
coils like a caduceus around
the kitchen sill. A fisted root
anchors the plant that feeds
on the swill in a chipped teacup.

Though the golden wreath has faded
from the hand-painted china,
the Red Dragon of Wales still
spans its scarlet wings.

With a raised front foot,
it too is pointing—back
through the leafy glass
at the steam spitting bricks
of the drycleaning plant.

Wherever there is mist
the gods are present.

THESE ARE THE DESCENDING CURRENTS

I know what beasts there are
at the bottom of the sea.
— Taliesen

At first, pastoral ancestors
slapped their coarse fibers
in the cataracts of Mount Snowdon;

conquered, they crawled in darkness,
ripping coal from the English pits;

one cave-in survivor crossed
in steerage to newfound servitude
in North Ohio mines;

his middle daughter married
into a family of drycleaners;

her husband's rages and consumptive
death, her suicide from melancholia
and crippling arthritis;

their sons ran the drycleaning shop,
battling over methods and money;

the postwar business boom too soon
sucked under by the synthetic riptides
of drip-dry, permapress, and modacrylic:

These were the descendant currents.
Why is such wet work called "dry"?

GRAMPA THOMAS

(Joseph Dafydd Thomas)

He escaped the coal mines by winning
an Eisteddfod in front of Queen Victoria.
"If I'm prized, I'll come up the mountain
waving a white handkerchief," he said
and he did. My aunt told me this story,
how singing brought him to America.

How when he was old in Ohio,
my Dad would fetch him home drunk
from Evans' bar. Grampa's voice waving
Main Street, singing "Mentra Gwen."
*Come, fairest Gwen, the stars in heaven
are bright, lady mine, lady mine.*

THE NAPHTHA

The gabardine phantom of my pants
-presser-father has landed
in the lampshade livingroom.
He's changed from the burial suit
into his usual garb, a battered
jacket with sheepskin lining.
I watch him fold this over
the davenport, crown the arm
with the brown felt fedora.
The naphtha from the cleaning
plant has settled in my eyes.

Dad pulls a stubborn pencil
from his left workshirt pocket,
tackles its point with a pearl
handled fishing knife. I hear
the rapid rub of graphite,
his baritone hum. Leaning
further from the doorframe,
I strain to read the page.
And it's only my fingers
that keep me from falling.

DRYCLEANERS

My father walks in clouds
leans into pillars of steam.
The lyre front radio cracks
gospel and weather inside
this windy chamber where racks
clash-clang hanger anvils
and Dad whistles naphtha.
The mayor's swallowtail
blimps on the steamform,
ghost snakes writhe through
stitch holes. Clang-slam
hiss-hang, the cloud gang
pins little pink tickets
on country club tuxes,
chiffon stoles for Order
of the Eastern Star.
Mrs. Foster's gold brocade
with real rhinestones on
the cuffs shoots rainbows
on maroon choir robes
somber in organpipe rank.
"I dreamt I dwelt in marble
halls," Dad serenades in mist.

THE CONDUCTOR

On the plywood countertop, Dad
turned out the customers' pockets,
sorted coins, matches, rubber safes.
A soapbox caught the red spent
cartridges he found in the flaps
of plaid wool hunting jackets.

In and out of the racks he darted
through plastic-bagged raiment
that hid him like blinds. Then
all I could see were his fingers
on hangers, the scuffling wingtips.

Dad's arms rose and fell
on the steam presser lid,
on the cistern pump at the back
of the cleaning plant, and *forte*
on the chipped piano keys
of our nextdoor cloudy house.

Always his motion of coming down
and the sounds of water, steam,
a polonaise.

DOWN BELOW

(the out building of the drycleaning plant)

Made of cinder block and windowless
its ceiling was festooned with ropes
hung from salvaged galvanized pipes.

Here carpets swung and were scrubbed
—runners from church aisles,
orientals of bankers and doctors.

Out back of Down Below, concrete
vats lay open and a white crust
covered the dumping pit.

When filled with rainwater,
an oil slick seeped through
the scab in iridescent pools.

Once I dragged a maple branch
into that swill, saw its rainbow
eat the bark, with a sizzle
swallow sticks.

UNDER A CRUCIFORM OF PAPER ROSES

The seamstress sets her coffee cup
on the walnut slabs of the spool
cabinet and threads the bobbin
on her Singer. With swift
scarred fingers she stitches
crimson lining into an old coat.

Its satin luster fills the lamplit
corner, and a violet sheen enamels
her bending figure until she too
gleams like the Pietá on her holy
medal that taps-taps the armature
with each tilting of the treadle.

THE CARPET

                    slick as shadows
slipped under the rug room door,
shot up the alley to hover
at the window. Its flowers
flashed in the neon red
ESTAB 1889 sign and scarlet
fringes dusted the sidewalk,
When the pink beam struck
the board-bound ledger,
Dad blinked, rushed aboard
the craft. Je-sus Savior
Pilot Me he sang to the tinny
moons of Perry Street.

Gliding by the Presbyterian,
he tipped his hat to the Lions
meeting in the turret room,
and just when the pep band
began forming monograms,
Dad buzz-bombed the playing
field. When he loopy-looped
the library, he saluted Great
Bookers arguing Aristotle.
Catching their updraft,
Father's forelocks stood
in question marks.

Climbing the clean singing air,
he knelt on blue paisley,
a cluster of roses, fists
holding fast the dandelion
borders. Suspenders x-ed
Dad's back like a kite skeleton.

Suddenly as the fringe slapped
a flying red horse over Mac's
gas station, the carpet careened,
peeled back to the cleaning
plant, pitched the pilot

into a moonless alley, then
slithered to its hangar.

Dad heard its tangled tassels
drag dead leaves until
at last it lay asleep
by the lampblack boiler
that looms in the rug room
larger than a jinn.

RECLAMATION

The suit salesman brought in
a powder blue dinner jacket.

It had belonged to my sister's
classmate Gerry who just got

stabbed in a pool hall.
Dad sponged the blood with

tepid water and ammonia.
The salesman kept saying,

"That coat ain't paid for yet
and I'm not gonna get stiffed."

THE SPOTTING BOARD

Narrower than an ironing sleeve
it reached over the slate top
of the sorting table. His nose
over this silver padded peninsula,

Dad surveyed each stained necktie
or lapel, then picked vials from
a box where boar bristle brushes
soaked in wide mouth canning jars.

Father swabbed the fabric nap
with carbon tetrachloride,
then flattened the garment
on the coffin-handled steam press.

He would ride its iron pedals
like Old Smoky in the freightyard
until its wheezing jaws spurted
cumulus to the pipe maze ceiling-sky.

There cloud stains became
the trade routes where silverfish
discovered continents and
waterbugs conducted governments.

THE TICKING

Sunrays, roses, roosters, crosses:
the aunts embroidered muslin
pillow slips for Mom and Dad.

Nature pictures tried to hide
that flattened feathered thing
in dark striped ticking,
smells of naphtha, mentholatum.

He'd slather camphorated salve
on chest and throat, hoping
to stop the cough, slow the nose
bleeds that spotted brown
a flossy cloud or bluebird wing.

Sweat, steam, medicine, machines
until flowers nest at last
on the gray November grass.

STEAM DUMMY

Ssssssssssssssssst there!
In the brick niche of the alley,
see the narrow pipe? Come peer
into that squint, come witness
my soliloquy:

I am Steam Dummy.
My heart is a bellows,
brain a boiler. I've clanging
lever limbs and pedal feet.
Sightless, yet my apertures
are legion. They whistle
and weep, hiss and can sing.
       I swear by Orificium
       my many ears hear plenty!

When the sun catches the tin
of Anthony Steel Safety pins
I see their afterburn like
shooting stars, and when the pins
stick Liberty tickets
to collars and waistbands
I hear the two soft taps.
       Listen to that pen scratch
       ciphers in the grided ledger!

All records are writ herein,
for I myself am stationery,
and what you mistake for marbling
on my skin's an alphabet
of waterspots.
       Here on my chest
       are pictographs.

In fluorescent lamplight, the men
pull garments over my form and for
moments they see a prom queen,
lodge brother, hellfire preacher
or caped impresario.
Dark and sartorial, I puff

and blow till apparel billows
about my torso. Tattletale gray,
my fiberglas skin's stuffed
with army surplus batting,
sweating pipes. Even so,
in gold lamé I'm their one
and only *Hello to Hollywood
Cocktails for Two!*
> There's no hooch more cutting to the lungs
> than the lye cloud over a deep dye vat.

Trigger-man on the steam gun,
Bill bursts each spot then brushes
the fabric with a sandpaper tune.
He's like a stagehand who creates
the sound of downpour by sifting
salt on paper, or by thrashing
sheet metal, can orchestrate
the tempest!
> Tho white lightning can't compete
> with fumes from a barrel of benzine!

Sssssssay you, clothes make a man?
Vestum virum facit? Well, what
about the clothes without the man?
And after Eden's fall, who
stitched the first fabric?
Did patriarchal cloaks
smack and twist
on a desert clothesline?
> It's sleeveless arms
> that stoke my boiler.

When a full moon threads
its satin through the iron
clad windows, the whips and pods
of castor bean trees
wave finger patterns
over my chromium platform.

For hardening hearts, dimming the brain,
moonshine's no match for carbon monoxide.

Tree worshippers.
Bill says his Druid ancestors
raised a Red Dragon banner
to protect their native tongue:
"Four things endure forever.
The earth, sky, sea,
and the speech of the Cymry."
        Y Gwir yn erbyn y Byd.
        (This Truth against the World.)

Ssssssssssssssssummer and Winter,
down the wooden sluice,
coal trucks shoot anthracite
into the dragon furnace.
An iron lettered plate shades
its arrow tongued flames.
Still, I tell you, there is
a shining in the basement.
        One blast and you'll be
        Tatterdemalion!

Often I've wondered who stirred up
my essence, puddling my pig iron
in a white blast furnace.
Whose hands tended the stokehole,
fed me coke through a grate mouth?
Who parented my frame, ferried
and fastened it to the cleaning plant
floor? Who's made me station-ary?
A very ape of apertures?
The oracle of the orifice?
        O my tubes and distillations!
        Why, I'm a headless mummy!

Suppose some ancient Egyptians
soaked my wraps in secret plants,
stored my organs in canopic jars.

This *is* an embalming shop.
Aren't waterbugs scarab-like?
But we ain't got no ankh here.
No symbol for supernal life
in this stewpot!
>I'd like to carve a cartouche
>for our dying sovereign's name.

Sssssssssssssss.
The funeral director crossed
Bill's wrists, pinned the hands
to a gold leafed Bible.
The sleeves of the burial suit
hid his hieroglyphs of burns.
>Now they're still, this presser's
>arms, his finisher's fingers.

For oratory, the preacher chose
the scripture James Four Fourteen:
Whereas ye know not what shall
be on the morrow. For what is
your life but vapour, that
appeared for a little time
and then vanished away.

FACTS WRITTEN ON WATER

Dedicated to my brothers
Thomas Rees, John Weston, and William Brandon

GLITTERS

Down the tracks and past the city
limits, the country club rose over
the golf links. Silver security fences
with climbing ivy tried to hide
the El Dorados, Catalina swimsuits.

From the rural route, I fished ditches
for golfballs, sold them a quarter
apiece. Or sliced away their cratered
surface till rubber bands boiled like
nests of new hatched garter snakes.

POOL

In the municipal swimming pool, a long rope
divided the deep from shallow. Its striped
wooden floats were like Dad's fishing bobbers.
His jointed bamboo poles had eyelets to
thread the floppy twine, while steel spinning
reels on Fiberglas rods whirred in the nylon
line. Mother-of-pearl lures shimmered
their silver barbs next to tinsel flies
which flickered in the army-black tackle box.
Its hinged trays were divided like Mom's
jewelry case, and they displayed minnows
of articulated mirrors, notched lead sinkers
caught up in bunches. Dad kept bloodworms,
nightcrawlers, alive in wet moss compost
mixed with sawdust. After warm long rains,
he turned over the soft loam, picked wrigglers
from the clay clods, then planted them
in a bait box of pressed cork. I preferred
bread crumbs—to halve the impalements.
Did lightningbug phosphorous continue to glow
under the lake—or did this bait become
bobbing lanterns inside the fishes' bellies?

In the municipal swimming pool, underwater
at night I'd hold my breath, stroke and stare
at the convex lamps. Larger than dinner plates,
their white radiance ribboned the green chlorine.
Monday mornings, Mom hauled watery garments
in an oval wicker basket to the back lot.
Clothespins in her teeth, she'd shake each sheet,
stretch and clamp those billowing bed sails.
Towels, shirts followed, hung on a plastic
-coated rope to bleach in the sun.

In the municipal swimming pool, I'd stretch
over the missing middle rungs, climb to
the concrete raft. Always before jumping
from that painted jade island, I'd hesitate,
attentive to the public address system.
Pouring down the sounds of the top-forty

hits, the deejay's tipsy voice purred
encoded dedications. I waited, dateless,
to hear my secret name in some rock-n-roll
crescendo. And in the canvas curtained bath
house, combed rats from my dripping hair.
Still listening to the p.a., I studied
my bony frame, bloodshot eyes, in the mirror
of pink lipstick letters and hearts.

RESERVOIR WATER TOWER

Our City Fathers smashed its metal shell,
so only this granite base remains where
clinging green creepers net the narrow
windows, hide the hand-hewn blocks.

In highschool, Dad and Uncle Rayleth
climbed its iron ladder side. Quoting
Romeo and Banquo's ghost, their phrases
floated over our town's waterworks.

Thee's and thou's sank to sediment tanks
and Juliet's praises skimmed the sludge
beds. Today an amputated turret profiles
the horizon of North Vine Street.

Where limestone mortar crumbles, pigeons
nest in niches. They ascend to the ancient
balcony and, sailing from the timeworn
railing, circle and dive the chopped summit.

ERIE

Phosphorescence sprays the black morass
as arthritics kick the glittering surface.
And, claiming minerals will cure contagion
or remold the body, comsumptives swim
the brackish wash.

Glaciers gouged Erie's shallow bowl.
It's the blow and tilt from gales,
the weight of water on its walls,
or from full-moon's pull, that once
a year makes the Lake turn over.

Propped in sling chairs, the more infirm
nest in shallows while the palsied lie
ashore on blankets, joints wrapped
in sand packs. All avoid the open Lake,
for they fear these freakish things:

The quick carriage of undertows,
the sudden long wave called *seiche*.
Some have seen whole islands covered,
coal and grain freighters crushed,
they know of torn hulls sucked down
and all hands lost.

THE ROMANCE OF DROWNING

We've imagined it: these bereaved
still breathing yet balletic,
accompanied by frolicking dolphins.

Or viewed from brookside, their
ghostly float of soaked drapery,
tendrils entwined in lilies, etcetera.

Not the blue bloated torsos,
faces frenzied from fish teeth,
nor the beach-heaps cloaked

in iridescent fly wings. Who
will know the faceless ones?

FACTS WRITTEN ON WATER

(A Play for Tour Guide and Poet,
The Blue Hole, Castalia, Ohio)

The most extraordinary spring
in existence, its depth is unknown.
> It is known that each bedouin tribe
> has a fear-cup engraved with prayers
> and crafted from the purest silver.
> Drink water from this cup
> and all fear leaves the heart.

Visible depth is forty-five feet.
Seventy-five feet in diameter.
> A metre of infant's urine is distilled
> for restorative potions. Some seek
> healing in purges of water mixed with wine.

Fish cannot live in the Blue Hole.
The water contains no food or air
and is extremely clear.
> Clear elixir of tears or pearls
> dissolved in vinegar is prescribed
> for the love-sickness water
> cannot quench. The faithful
> journey to the sacred rivers.

Looking down, we see the Blue Hole
open like a morning glory.
> Glory-halleluiah in the Ganges or Jordan.
> Their book of holy writ flows
> in fountains of living water,
> torrents of the cataracts.

Dye-markers reveal the water's
source is an underground river.
> Rivers that map the heart's yearning
> for the water brooks. In the grave
> we won't recall rainfall or the sink
> and glide of fish under the water's glass.

The temperature is forty-eight degrees
whether winter or summer.
                    Winter or summer we won't recollect
                    which kittens drowned in rainbarrels
                    or FACTS WRITTEN ON WATER:
                    drip of lime forms stalactites;
                    ground water is half-mile under surface;

The Blue Hole discharges
five-thousand gallons
of water every minute.
                    every minute prisoners water tortured;
                    water in our atmosphere ten times
                    as large as in all rivers;
                    no liquid oxygen or water on Mars;

This phenomenon was discovered by
Robert Rogers in Seventeen-Sixty.
                    in Sixteen-sixty only slaves
                    were dyers, Quakers wore white;
                    ancient Romans invented aqueducts.

In Nineteen-sixty while releasing
dye markers, a diver was lost.
                    Lost forever, Vincent's basin
                    and pitcher in the bedroom at Arles;
                    Sherwood Anderson forever bereft
                    of the waterworks of Clyde.

The diver was a victim of
nitrogen narcosis, more commonly
called Raptures of the Deep.

                    (Poet and Guide in Unison)
                    Deep is the heart's yearning
                    for the water brooks
                    inside the morning glory
                    where the fish have no eyes
                    drink water from this cup
                    and all fear leaves the heart.

PERCHES

For William Meredith

Still wrapped in water, a hooked perch
was flipping stripes on the cutting table.
Hand-held pliers hammered the head.
The gill and fin tympanny began to still
before scraped away scales flew like metal
chips—then a quick slit, lifting out the cord.

Each day at work, mail came wrapped in a cord.
The innocent envelopes placed on their perch
in pigeon-holes of gray painted metal.
Paper fins lay flat, gills slit on the table
top where I unfolded black and white still
photographs shot inside Chile, hidden to head

For Mexico. The microfilm flew in thunder head
clouds to Washington, D. C., to where the cord
was opened. I unfolded the AMNESTY NEWS still
ignorant of "La Parotta," the parrot's perch.
It reported a poet's arrest at the kitchen table
where her children cried and threw their metal

Cups, spoons, and grabbed at the soldier's metal
handcuffs, nightstick, and how he hit each head
and back save for a baby hidden beneath the table.
He dragged their mother to the van, tied a cord
of wires on her wrists—then told her the perch
would make her talk, La Parotta keep her still,

Stripped and manacled to the t-shaped bar, still
dripping water, she tried to balance on the metal
bands. Guards with cattle prods stood by the perch,
called her a trade-union-shit and beat her head
and feet. Photographs to monitor the spinal cord
and electroshock somehow got left on a cafe table.

Near the Villa Grimalde prison, a film can on a table
held photos of her face: a before of disbelief, still
frames of screams and starings, how one distorted cord

of mouth and neck cry out children's names. Metal
scrapes manacles of hate, prods that burn the head,
will sear the soul: La Parotta, Chile, parrot perch.

Photos left on a table, electroshock on metal, a torso
still suspended keeps screaming in my head—no it's not
a cord of fishes, but a poet strung from a perch.

THE SHEAVES

Dedicated to Linda Manick and Marie Koury

SHEAVES

(The Books Speak)   *(The Corn Speaks)*

Tropic of Cancer, Revolutionary
Non-Violence & The Holy Bible

There is no word for the sound
of cornstalks rubbing in rows

rubbing through covers
their spines touch

for the breathing of leaves the
thresher has cut my ears away

my author sought the street
life my stitcher sang gospel

I hear crickets still rubbing
their legs in volumes

my writer is a pacifist alone
my binder raised her children

they hum honeysuckle sounds
inside corn silo columns

my maker walked on water
my cutter lost a thumb

OFFICE FOR THE DEAD

Born of a woman, hath
but a short time to live.

From the backseat of our '49 Chevy
I see phonelines of starlings
move the blue Ohio sky. "At your age,"
my driving Mother tells me, " I had
two dresses, I'd wear one, wash
the other. That was The Depression."
I explain my gray blazer, its two pair
of dress pants I wear to the office,
and "the other secretaries so magazine-cute
you'd never guess we're having
a great depression." I wake up,
see my cats on my bed in reversed nines.

We fade away suddenly
like the grass.

Thirty paper stacks to staple,
I march about the table
collating columns. I know
the old poets made their words
winged like nightingale cries
or purple-vaulted skies.
Still I must make a living
piling other people's words.
Tonight I'll write this
triplet in my white ruled
single subject pad:
O trees today I collate
your pieces recalling
the green peace of your limbs.

Fleeth as it were a shadow.

I know you secretaries
'cause I'm your carbon copy
and you're mine. I know
how that awful ache

makes you reverse letters
and skip lines.

Of whom shall we seek for succor?

You used to smile as you passed
in the hallway: two char women
in green housekeeping uniforms.
Your eyes saw me—secretary
at a fat desk, someone else to
yes ma'am, sitting on her
white ass at a cushy desk job.
Next time you look you'll laugh
at my paperclip coat of mail,
my grenades of photocopier
cartridges, stamped BULK RATE
PRINTED MATTER warpaint.
Now is the time for all good
to brandish feather dusters,
toilet brushes, Snowbowl molotov
cocktails with flaming tampon
fuses. We charge! Throw paper
hurricanes up and down the halls.
See how floppy diskette pylons
hover   crash   land
on the president's sunset desk!

Earth to earth.

Memorandum to H. D. Thoreau:
Though she will never have
the leisure to observe
a battle between ants
or write on the geographic
location of heaven,
yet any clerk typist
could give you lessons on
"...life is frittered
away by detail."

Ashes to ashes. Dust to dust.

Yes lust teases me at my desk.
No matter which way I turn
clothes rub my skin lonesome
for your touch. An awful hunger
squeezes lungs, presses intestines
against each other. The lab chart
on the wall reminds me of your
anatomy, so my fingers type
furiously to sublimate
this passion, my obsession
to watch you write your name
on paper, walk on river wall.
Refract within me glass and
water I cannot comprehend...

Looking for the life
of the world to come.

On the train I wait, anticipate
your certain carriage, secret beauty
bursting through pneumatic doors.
Darling. Never thought I'd write
that word. But cliched soldiers
have invaded the car shooting off
their sticky mouths my sweet
honeyluv. I turn toward windows.
I must reflect on inventory:
duplicator fluid, felt tip pens,
liquid paper and reinforcements.

At whose second coming
to judge the world.

Emily, you wrote, "This
is my letter to the world,"
and I know, having typed millions,

how in your space where
no one could erase or
smear it you could make
your mark. Today a fly
buzzed in this office
that's got no window.

Deliver us not into eternal death.

Observe if for its shape
the weight is excessive,
look for oil, grease, sweet
or sour odors. Feel for
springiness, stiffness,
look for lumps. Be attentive
to title errors of officers,
organizations. Was this
an odd method of delivery?
from unknown foreign origin?
Watch for overage of postage,
seriously regard directions
(to be only opened by...).
Beware of any string, wire,
plastic or protruding foil.
Do not handle unnecessarily.
Isolate the object beneath
an open window. Evacuate
employees from the immediate
vicinity. Dial nine-one-one.
Notify authorities.

*Blessed are they that
die in the Lord.*

Carolyn Johnson, I am
the secretary sent to take
your place. Your glasses
and cupcakes are still
in your drawer and I write
this with your pen.
One workday I saw you—

fifty shaky smoking too
much too overweight too
lonely. One afternoon
you left the office alone
went home alone and heard,
you even died alone in your
apartment. It was two days
before they found you filed
under A (Alone). I'm done
transcribing your notes,
typing finals from the drafts.
Carolyn Johnson, who says
women can't be drafted?
We're already drafts—rough
copy onionskin foolscap
manifold carboncopy throw
away get another tissue
typewriter secretary wife.
I take a clean sheet of paper
roll it in the carriage
center your name:
                    Carolyn Johnson.
Carol, I'm all keyed up and
I feel it in my bonds in my tissues
in my correctype liquidpaper brain.
Say after breathing whiteout
mimeofluid typecleaner thirty (30)
years were you high when you died?
I'm glad you were cremated,
not filed in a drawer under
any watermarked engraved
letterhead, Carolyn Johnson.
Stop.
Reach out fingers on the home
rows deathrows of this world
touch home touch my face touch
Carolyn's ashes somewhere
in Pennsylvania touch away
machinated lives mere extensions
of machines clicking tapping thudding
like tiny nails in coffin lids like

ticking clocks in mausoleumed
office buildings like touch comma
and release us from margins comma
like clear tabs capitalize your
period don't reset space bar
lock shift index return return
return Carolyn Johnson.

For they shall rest
from their labours.

Like a Ripley's cartoon my typed
pages could reach to the moon
and back. Believe it or not,
I can see my highschool-self
in pony tail and penny loafers
reciting in a kinda stammer:
"...on the shore of the wide
world I stand alone and think.
Till love and fame
to nothingness do sink."

We shall not all sleep
but we shall all be changed.

A thousand years in Thy sight
is but a twinkling of an eye.
Thus spake harp-king David.
Sans stereo components,
shepherds move lightly,
a few skins, stones, while
rulers have it rougher,
whole kingdoms by camel caravan.
Grandma had the same house
sixty years. Two bedrooms
with coral bell paper
upstairs. Acrosonic spinnet,
shawl backed sofa, down.

"Don't ever give up your home,"
she said, always assuming I'd own.

O Jerusalem, how I long
to take you under my wing.
Come into my fortress
or twined and piled books
where under a mattress buttress
cats are camels that rest
on piles of rejected manuscripts.
Outside, under a moving moon,
the whole world swirls
in wars, in revolutions.
While this new poem wobbles,
spins, a steady gyroscope
on its sure string.

"NO LOITERING WASHING SMOKING"

Here in the women's lavatory
(from the Latin, a room for washing)

she kneels at the toilet lid
lined up with bottles, bangles,

and at that strange altar
in its triptych of stalls

Solemnity plaits her hair
with incense pomade

(her arms moved slowly
like wings.)

GREAT OAKS HOME POEM

We need a poet to create sestinas
for the middle-aged lady
with a mental age of six, raped
repeatedly by institution orderlies.

And a poet to pen a ballad
for an unnamed man with a "tendency
to stuff objects in his mouth."
A doctor's glove was found
lodged in the trachea.

Perhaps rhyming couplets for Brenda
dead from seizure, her head stuck
between the bed rails? She was
"always trying to get
into small places."

Only six months here and Robert's
lost every skill from his six years
of special schooling. Can we have
some free verse here?

Poet, compose a sonnet for Stephen
who vomits fourteen times a day.
His caretaker reports tonight Steve
has smiled—for the very first time.

A LITTLE ELEVATION

Dedicated to my mother
Ida Elizabeth

PLAIN FANCY

Westward it was landlocked, flat as haddocks.
So prairie families fled to county fairs
for ferris wheels, raced rattletrap Fords
over molehill bridge abutments—anything
for a little elevation!

Yet, as they slept, cowbarns stretched
to castle shadows, corn silos rose
to skyscraper shapes. Under moonlight,
the plowed fields looked like lakes
and fireflies their blinking freighters.

PORTRAIT OF A PACKER

(For Gale S.)

In bitter winter or in hundred degree heat
she'd leave our street in red plaid jacket,
bluejay overalls, earflaps cap. In waterproof
boots, she took the shortest route, cutting
up alleys to the clapboard slaughterhouse.
Punching the timeclock propped on the pork
renderings barrel, she crossed the curing room
of hanged hogs, passed thru the stainless steel
doorway of the packing cooler. She stood up
her whole shift, picking paraffin coated boxes
off the conveyer, quickly filling them with rows
of sausages, then sealing the cellophane folds
with a hot rod-iron. At lunchtime, she dragged
a lard pail past the gravel lot to the only maple.
Her back against bark, she savored java, spam,
sometimes sang Glenn Miller tunes: *String of
Pearls* and *Little Brown Jug*. She knew music
was taboo, the company radio used for noontime
livestock news or Cleveland Indians ballgames.
"Moonlight becomes you, it goes with your hair,
you certainly know the right thing to wear,..."

READING *THE NEW YORKER*

(For Sharon Cumberland)

Each Christmas Uncle Howard sent
subscriptions for *Sports Afield* or
The Saturday Evening Post. Still
Mother pillaged the library racks,
bringing home *Harpers* and *Vogue*.

Pushing back the red-letter Bible
she'd stack these eastern splendors
on our Ohio tabletop of fake paper
marble, eclipsing coffee rings.

There my bobbysocks toed the midwest
table ledges and my skirt pleats
propped a metropolis of dreams
when, ignoring the chores or 4-H finals,
I hummed and thumbed through *The New Yorker*.

Under its slick pale cover, black cats
proclaimed Sin beneath an edict that
diamonds are eternal, while a perfumed
lady with her violin-lover humped
andante down the piano bench.

In tweeds and buns, black and white ads
strolled in their sensible shoes.
Plungeneck vamps smoked with silver
holders opposite showtimes,
poems in champagne letters.

Stark in that sparkle, I saw us
in the cartoons of workers with beaks.
Laundry lines drooped from our ceiling.
A monkey wrench stood in our soup.

MOON LIFE

(Tercets on a musician mother)

Mother Ida, I hear your voice,
see your face in mirrors.
            Put a little light on the subject.

Your highschool annual predicted you'd
be a photographer for the *New York Sun*.
            Let's just wait and see.

A career gal who'd marry big,
a society-page lady.
            There's cold in them-thar hills.

The only time you made the paper
was by having another baby.
            Them's that has gets.

I can see maps at the backs of your legs
where all you rivers go.
            Down by the riverside...

You were always pouring over Edna Millay,
The New Yorker, Vogue.
            All the news that's print to fit.

You're not impressed
with -ism or -ologies.
            We had one too but the wheels came off.

I think you make your music
what you never speak or weep of,
            Come to me my melancholy baby....

The organ's tremulous waves
piano's rippled quietude.
            Thank you Mrs. Zilch.

I always speculate
on the singing you accommodate.
                You win the fur-lined bathtub.

Lead Kindly Light, Palestrina,
Battle Hymn of the Republic
                Clean up your plates.

How long have mothers been like moons
to their daughters,
                one side never seen?

CLOSET POEM

In dim winter light, the walls
were archaeological strata:
rose trellis era, then
quill-scroll period over
scratched plaster neolithic.

The linoleum too was layered
with a fake parquet peeking
through cracked congoleum rug.

Among the cartons of bombazine
and moth crystals lay a suitcase,
its black acetate worn
down to the brown backing.

I unsnapped its brass clasps,
lifted out the flowered frock
Mom got married in. Slowly
I unfolded the soft serge,
when from its skirt fell
snapshots of old school chums.

Under these was a mounted poem,
its stanzas entwined by roses
and pickets. I can still tell you
its last line: Purity and humility
will make every girl a queen.

CEILINGS

In Ohio we slept on spoolwood bedsteads,
contemplating ceiling cracks and x-ray visions:
how over plaster-rafter-tile, stars shifted
their pictures.

Like a page from Uncle Wiggly's puzzle book,
those planetoid pets in dot-to-dot reached
Paris, Rome, even Ceylon. We knew Big Bear
hovered over

New York City where, behind doorchains
bolted top to bottom, Great Aunt Harriet
decked in diamonds, dined on Delmonico steak,
sipped sparkley.

TRAPEZE

(Melzer Thomas)

There were no nets in the sawdust
rings during the Depression
when Dad's Cousin Melzer
did the triple somersault.

The son of Welsh immigrants,
he italianized his given name,
became The Flying Melzorri
for John Ringling North.

Later in the Fifties
when wizened in a wheelchair,
Melzer came to visit with
a young bleached blonde wife.

Every time she pushed his chair
her bangle bracelets slid and
glittered. How she loathed
our northern climate, hated
staying in trashy trailerparks.

Back when the Big Top wintered
in Florida, she and The Signore
once owned a cunning bungalow
where yellow cascades of orchids
graced the palm tree patio.

Perfect timing, said Cousin Melzer,
that's the secret of the triple.
The flyer must know exactly
when to break out of the third.

THE GRADE SCHOOL I ATTENDED
WAS NEXT TO A SLAUGHTERHOUSE

How do you like to go up in a swing,
Up in the air so blue?
Oh, I do think it the pleasantest thing
Ever a child can do!
                                        -Robert Louis Stevenson

My feet pass cupola, weathercock,
touch nimbus clouds over Holmes
School. Chainsaw spurt-squeals,
pigs screaming, I know I must
go higher to make these rusty
swingchains outshout death.

                    *

Too scared for sex, so my beau
pumped me standing up in swings.
April sprang its stars over
Holmes School, the animals asleep,
we hummed in chains.

BIOLOGY I

Coach chloroforms the hen.
A cotton wad soaked in fumes
sends the room spinning.
He opens the flipchart to
Cross-View of the Heart's
Four Chambers: Ventricle,
Auricle, Left, Right.

We gather, see the muscle tick-
tock. In-out, a perfect pump,
open-close. "And now," he says,
"the sacrifice, from the Latin,
sacrificium." And pouring ether
through stuffed beak, we see
the clock slow. Stop.

QUO VADIS?

Miss Malone began Latin by explaining
some phrases those Romans bequeathed us.
"Tempus fugit," she'd say, tapping black
slate with poplar wood pointer. A smack
on the doorsills indicated *"porta"* and
arcs toward the windows explicated *"fenestra."*
Each year ended with a May *Saturnalia.*

In the gymnasium, stacked sewer pipes wrapped
in white newsprint were striped and scrolled,
Ionic-style. Canvas wrestling mats, lent
by Coach, lay unrolled on the villa floor.
He as Caesar and Miss Malone as Portia
wore *stolas* and weeping willow laurels
twisted through their glasses' temples.

At that Latin Banquet, first year pupils
played slaves. We freshmen stood in back
or carried trays laden with concord grapes
and garlic bread to reclining sophomores.
In this tableau of bedsheet togas, towel
tunics, we poured sodapop in tin prop
goblets for Senators and Patrician ladies.

They seemed so resplendent in their purple
crepe paper trim and laughing at Coach's
halting recitation of "The Frogs."
Beneath the banner, S.P.Q.R., Miss Malone
quoted Catullus and for the hundredth time
told of Romulus and Remus. I flunked
Freshman Latin so stayed a slave.

OHIO SONG CYCLE

Eavesdropping

Lightningbugs, crickets.
The Big Bear spun
over the dark shadowed house.
Children couched
in lily-of-the-valley
watch the play:
mothers, aunts, uncles,
icetea and cigarettes.

Heavenly Bodies

At first crack we
were stars: hunter, queen,
swan, dog, our ancestors.
Mrs. Mottram was a Gold Star
Mother, so we always took
her serious. The piano
teacher stuck them on
sheet music, and Grandma
would exclaim, "My Stars!"

Stars and Stripes

In Ohio it snowed on Halloween
parades of high school bands,
city council cars. One year
my cousin wore a monkeysuit,
danced with dyed-longjohn
Ubangi, and while conducting
Sousa's march, the V.F.W. band
director died of a heart attack.
Folks said it was "fitting"
since music was his glory.
We always stopped by Grandma's
for popcorn balls and cider.

Cider Mill at Amsden

The old station wagon hugged
October country roads past
farms, white churchyards
to a little valley shack
of cold wet timbers.
Apples bruised our feet
in the yard—the air
coldsweet as a grave.

Largo

Lost, lonely in procession,
file the aisles past grownup pews.
Mr. Sailyers lifts his fiddlebow,
Old Man Ketchum hums bullfiddle,
and the Sunday school orchestra
strikes up *Jesus Loves Me.*
Handel's *Largo* follows.

Preparation for Decoration Day

My Grandma high up cemetery hill
calls out names of the dead:
"Bobby, Anna, Theophilus."
Deliberate in old ladies shoes
she directs us with a trowel:
"Tom, Chris, Elizabeth,
put hollyhocks babies breath
Vanfleet roses in them coffeetins
bottles and jars."

Pelton's Quarry

Mudbank to opposite, swim fast
the springfed ice depths,
fear the scrape of tree branch,

muskrat tail, submerged fossil
secrets whispering warnings:
car parts, weapons, broken
bodies lodged inside
niagara shale ledges.

A.M.

Morning milk horses, ghosts now,
pull the Union Dairy Company wagon.
Their hollow hooves echo precise
as scales, pressing the buckeye
blossoms and leaves. Angel steam
from their snouts brings dawn
down Fremont Street.

I DREAM OF DAD DEAD AGAIN

We're out on our latticed back porch.
Grass edgers, bamboo rake, and rusty spade
hang on jagged nails over old newspapers
bundled for the boyscout scrap drive.

"I'm a poet now," I explain myself
over a burst bag of Huron cement.

Dad's lips crack and his jaw, twenty-five
years silent, loosens its fossils:
"Homer, Milton, Tennyson.
Dai Thomas is the only good modern."
Our green and dying arms embrace.

"Wait," I say, but too late.
He fades into criss-crossed light.

BANDAGES BRING LIGHT

Dedicated to my husband
William Edward Bordley

CANIS MAJOR

(Megan, a Guide Dog)

The bus seat is low, so you must stay
flat, head turned to fit under footrest.
Black silhouette on yellow linoleum,
you keep vigil in this chrome striped
vinyl home until in candy bunny pose
you snooze, chase bristly critters
clean up mountaintop. At cliffside
you spring, leap-lope through clouds
in a harness of stars. Lady Sirius,
your master arcs beside you, with
slighted Orion you orbit the Earth.

LEARNING RUSSIAN WITH MY BLIND LOVER

I flash the cards English-side in:
Say "Seaside. Flower. Cloud."

You speak: "Morskee. Svehtak.
Oblaka—that's clouds. They're not like
a star or sun that has a certain shape.
Each cloud's different, moves around.
I remember faces of my family, roses,
tulips, and those kind you blow on.
Just once I'd like to see an owl,
watch its sudden swoop, chest-feathers
rattling, hoo-hoo in moonlight."

I hand you the wordcards.
You hold them upside down.

ARE THE STARS OUT TONIGHT?

Back before your blindness, little silver
minnows swarmed the rural Delaware night,
hovered a halo over your Mom frying cabbage,
her iron skillet singing rainfall,
I don't care if it's cloudy or bright.

*

The first apparition came by daylight,
a purple rectangle with jagged edges
floated in your left field of vision.
The moon may be high, but I can't
see a thing in the sky.

*

Your Mom described the Jersey side, the shape
of Lady Liberty. From the Greyhound tinted
windows, you saw raw sunlight, how it bounced
from the Hudson to the shores of Massachusetts
General. *Cause I only have eyes for you, dear.*

*

Etherized maples, scarlet in the schoolyard,
sang BANDAGES, BRING LIGHT, while shining
cornshocks bowed like pharoah's Bible story.
A radio banged its harp on the high iron
bed rails. *I don't know if we're in a garden....*

*

Later at state institute, you took
mobility skills, Braille training.
With slate/stylus pickax, you dredged
diplomas from academic caverns.
... or on a crowded avenue,

*

Flat as a flounder, the guide dog lay under
the subway seat. First I spotted a tail,
then your quick fingers fathoming dots.
We talked of groundhog weather. *You are here,*
so am I, maybe millions of people go by.

*

We wore roses in the courthouse, wired
red carnations to your guide dog's harness.
Next pledged troth, took good luck stuff
from family, friends, signed statistics
registry. *But they all disappear from view.*

*

A dozen holidays dissolved, our daughter
stroked to shore. Tonight we're dervishes
spinning a hot waltz, while this deejay
blasts that golden olden. Baby, it's all
true, *Cause I only have eyes for you.*

[Credit: "I Only Have Eyes For You," words by Al Dubin,
music by Harry Warren, (c) 1944 by Remick Music Corp;
copyright renewed.]

HEATWAVE

Nude, dripping with cats
we lay facing the floor fan,
recalled long ago science lessons
how hot air is molecules rapidly
rubbing and pressing each other.

It was the same every Friday.
In school we sat in dark rows
facing the screen, waiting
for the zitskin boy from
the Projectionist Club
to thread, spin the film.

Reels clicking over amplified
barnyard sounds, a baritone
narrates "Predicting the Weather"
or "Reproduction in Hogs."
Flying cartoon arrows were
currents of air, or semen,
and the film always broke.

One day a stray ran in
from the street,
disrupting the movie,
shouting and barking.

EUTHANASIA

Master hoists you over his shoulders, carries
you down the apartment stairs to city sidewalk.
Splayfoot, cripple hipped, you scrape and splatter
on the slate pavement, rock-rocking in gimpy gait.
I follow, watch you stop to sniff the crabgrass,
chickweed, a picket fence—that makes you happy
—then we three reach the doctor's doorway.

In the waiting room we share a hundred licks,
kisses, nicknames, oh sweet killing words.
You slide on the stainless steel table
as doctor listens, probes, pronounces.
I stroke your coat that never fades from beauty,
nor the liquid imploring eyes.

Master gives a last embrace, doctor carries
torso while his assistant holds your paws
together as if at prayer. I watch you go
nose first through the dark doorway,
the tail through doctor's elbow goes last.
Singing pleas descend the cellar steps until
nothing is left but to write the check.

WINDOWS

By the violin sending windows, Carol was candling
the eggs. Embryos divided from unfertilized,
she singed feathers or lime spurs stuck to shells.
By the back stoop stood the silver painted pump,
the well water always acrid in rusty cup.
Stretched in trees, we sang our school song
in the lightningbug dusk, surrounded by
the feathered silhouettes of cornfields.

By the drive, the dark barn rose up cavernous,
its oaken doors opened to shadowed rafters.
Hooks, straps, black wires swayed like gallow
strings. Dad said, "That old man hamstrings
his livestock to geld them—uses no anesthetic
but a gag." Once I heard them, thrashing
and upside down, their bloodspurt
splattering the boards.

CHORES

Caroline told time by counting chores.
The seconds, eggs; minutes, milkcows;
cherries gather hours; everyday was
baking. Why, she canned the calendar!

Beneath the tin filigree ceiling
a pendulum clock tocked its lead locket.
Carol took up apron, rolled up sleeves
of her rayon frock, pulled on oxfords.

The hens were swung, vertebrae popped.
Caroline dunked each in steamy buckets.
Plucked them *staccato* as piano keys,
fuzz stuck to her dripping fingers.

Now the fowls were stripped, twisted
together. You've never see this?
How she snickered at my winces!
I was shoveling gravel from a truck

Bed, filling sink holes by the hen
house. Honeycomb windows, lightbulb
incubators, flats with quick chicks.
I had expected the cow barns.

The sod domed milk house, Caroline's
mousers preening in the treetops.
Lonesome for morsels, they stalked
in their stripes, in sunlight slept

On the corrugated coop roof. Carol's
bedstead had a goosefoot patterned
quilt, her cross-stitched pillows
showed seagulls, praying hands.

"WELSH CUSTOMS"

(An inscribed picture plate)

Just what were their habits,
these men in tailed coats,
women in tall hats, who walked
beside the gentry carriage?

Over the cobblestones, where
were they going? What did they
carry in knapsacks and satchels?
Who ferried the horse?

In the crown of the corner cupboard,
a hobnail held that plate upright
though often with a hammer knock
it fell on its faces.

A miracle it didn't break
from the crash of six children
slamming doors, racing to supper,
the eldest practicing *grands jetes.*

Or maybe that inscription said,
"Welsh Costumes." Did our Reeses
and Thomases wear such duds
when with blankets and baskets
they boarded the steerage?

A green swan, praying hands,
harness bells: the cupboard jumble
still sits in Mother's north Ohio
house. Where did the plate go?
No one can say.

FRAGMENTS FROM THE FIRE

The Triangle Shirtwaist Company Fire

March 25, 1911

Poems concerning the Triangle Fire
of March 25, 1911, are written
in memory of sisters who died in the
Fire—Bettina and Frances Miale,
Rosalie and Lucia Maltese,
Sara and Sarafine Sariciano—
and are dedicated to my sisters,
Sara Jane Reinhart and Elizabeth Ann James.

AUTHOR'S NOTE

The Triangle Shirtwaist Company manufactured blouses for women and was located on the eighth, ninth, and tenth floors of the Asch Building, at the corner of Washington Place and Greene Street, in New York City's Washington Square.

The company employed up to 900 workers at a time, but on March 25, 1911, only about 500 were present. These were immigrants, most of whom could not speak the English language. Nearly all were female, primarily Russian or Italian, although twelve nationalities were known to be "on the books."

At about 4:45 p.m., just after pay envelopes had been distributed, a fire broke out. Not everyone was able to reach the elevators and stairways. On the ninth floor, because the bosses had kept the doors locked to keep out union organizers, workers were forced to jump from windows. One hundred forty-six people, some as young as fourteen, perished.

This is doing a lot of work for the poems

To proclaim the acceptable year of the Lord;
to appoint unto them that mourn in Zion,
to give unto them beauty for ashes . . .
the garment of praise for the spirit
of heaviness.
—*Isaiah 61: 2, 3*

THE GREAT DIVIDE

Henry Street, Cherry Street, Hester Street:
the new world turns towards old Jerusalem.
Sunrays stream on the bearded father-singers
standing beside a hundred rag-stuffed windows.

Chant the "Havdallah," chant "The Great Divide."

They praise the Almighty for creating us a Sabbath
that cuts one day away from the fabric of the week.
Bent over Singers, their backs to factory windows,
women and children stitch into sunset.

Wait for the darkness, time for going home.

They piecework shirtwaists under the company sign—
the letters set in English, Hebrew, Italian:
"If you don't show up on Saturday or Sunday,
you've already been fired when it's Monday."

Chant the "Havdallah," chant "The Great Divide."

Still the sun drops, and the fathers pour
the ritual wine into a little platter.
Each strikes a sulphur-tip match, touches
the surface of the small wine lake.

Lights in the windows, dividing up the dark.

MARCH 25, 1911

It was Spring. It was Saturday.
Payday. For some it was Sabbath.
Soon it will be Easter. It was
approaching April, nearing Passover.
It was close to closing time.

The heads of trees budding
in Washington Square Park.
The sun a hot flywheel spinning
the earth's axle. The days long
enough for leaving in light.
                    It was Spring.   *— Location*

America's sweethearts—the ladies—
stroll in shirtwaists of lawn and lace,
mimic Charles Dana Gibson's Girls.
They pose in finery cut from bolts of
flimsy and stitched by garment girls
on Wilcox & Gibbs and Singer machines.
                    It was Saturday.

Up in the Asch Building
in the Triangle Shirtwaist Company
Rosie Glantz is singing "Every Little
Movement Has a Meaning of Its Own."
Fixing hair, arranging puffs and tendrils,
the other girls in the cloakroom join in:
"Let me call you Sweetheart,
I'm in love with you."
                    It was Payday.

Attar-of-roses, lily of the valley,
still they smell of machine oil
that soaks the motors and floors.
The barrel in each stairwell
could fill a thousand lamps.
                    For some it was Sabbath.

Here at Triangle, Sophie Salemi
and Della Costello sew on Singers.

Neighbors from Cherry Street,
they piecework facing each other,
the oil pan hitting their knees.
Tomorrow sisters will nail flowers
on tenement doors.

                   Soon it will be Easter.

The machine heads connecting the belts
to the flywheel to rotating axle
sing the Tarantella. Faster,
faster vibrate the needles, humming
faster the fashionable dance.

                   It was approaching April.

this is a stitch to locate, ground the reader

Della and Sophie up on Ninth
piece sleeves, race the needle's pace
not knowing on Eighth, paper patterns
burn from the wire, fall on machines,
spark moths and pinwheels round the room.
Rockets push up cutting-tables.

                   It was nearing Passover.

On Eighth, cutters throw pails of water
on the lawn of flame, and Louis,
holding the canvas hose, hollers:
"No pressure! Nothing coming!"

                   It was close to closing time.

Down on Greene Street, Old Dominick
pushes his wheelbarrow, describes
"a big Puff" when windows popped,
glittering showers of glass.

                   It was Spring.

Swords flaming, Pluto flies to Ninth.
Sophie and Della and dozens of others
jump on machine tables; the aisles jammed
with wicker workbaskets and chairs.

                   It was Saturday.

Mrs. Yaller testified: "Some froze at
machines. Others were packed in the cloakroom

filled with smoke. I heard them yelling
in Yiddish or Italian, crying out
the names of their children."
                    It was Payday.

Reporter Bill Shepherd is writing:
"I remember the great strike of last year,
these same girls demanding decent
working conditions."
                    For some it was Sabbath.

Rosie runs to the stairway. The door,
Locked! The telephone, Dead! Piling red
ribbons, fire backs girls into windows.
They stand on sills, see the room
a smashed altar lamp, hear the
screaming novenas of flame.
                    Soon it will be Easter.

Pleats of purple and gold wave,
incandescent filaments of lace snow
in shrapnel of needles and screws.
The blaze from molten bolts stains
glass, walls and lawns—on Cherry Street
sisters nail flowers on tenement doors.
                    It was approaching April.

"I could see them falling,"
said Lena Goldman. "I was sweeping out
in front of my cafe. At first some thought
it was bolts of cloth—till they opened
with legs! I still see the day
it rained children. Yes,
                    It was nearly Passover."

Sophie and Della stand on windowsill,
look out on the crazy quilt of town:
We will leave for our
block on Cherry Street,
leave these skeletons
leaning on machines,
the faces fixed on black
crucifix of cloakroom window.

It was close to closing time.

The *Times* quotes Mr. Porter: "The Triangle
never had a fire drill—only three factories
in the city have. One man I pleaded
with replied, 'Let em burn. They're
a lot of cattle anyhow.'"
                              It was Spring.

Sophie and Della stand on sill:
We will leave, our arms
around each other, our only
sweethearts. Piling red roses
two white hearses pull up
Cherry Street and the Children
of Mary Society march
in banners of prayers.
                              It was Saturday.

Captain Henry was the first policeman to arrive:
"I saw dozens of girls hanging from sills.
Others, dresses on fire, leapt from the ledges."
                              It was Payday. —> *creepy meaning*

Sophie and Della look on crazy quilt of town:
Fifty of our schoolmates
sing in procession
O Trinity of Blessed Light
Our Lady of Perpetual Help
Ave Maria, Ave Maria
Now and at the Hour
of the Tarantella.
                    For some it was Sabbath.

Ordering the nets and ladders, Battalion
Chief Worth explains, "I didn't know
they would come down three and even four
together. Why, these little ones went
through life-nets, pavement and all."
                    Soon it will be Easter.

Sophie and Della stand on windowsill:

Look, the flywheel sun sinks
in the west. In the Winter
Garden, Mr. Jolson springs
and bows in blackface.

It was approaching April.

At the Metropolitan Opera
George M. Cohan struts "The Rose
of Tralee" to the rich trailing
in diamond-sackcloth, rending
green ashes of dollar bills.

It was nearing Passover.

Sophie and Della stand on sill,
look down crazy quilt of town:
Intertwined comets we will stream
the nightmares of Triangle Owners
Joseph Asch
Max Blanck
Isaac Harris.

It was close to closing time.

Our Bosses of the Locked
Doors of Sweetheart Contracts
who in puffs and tendrils
of silent telephones,
disconnected hoses, barred
shutters, fire escapes
dangling in perpetual no
help on earth in heaven.

It was Spring.

The Lord is my Shepherd
green pastures still
waters anointest heads
with oil overflowing
preparest a table—now
our arms around each other
we thread the needle where
no rich man can go spinning
the earth's axle we are
leaving in light.

O Lord my God, thou art very great!
Thou art clothed with honor and majesty,
who coverest thyself with
light as with a garment,
who stretchest out the heavens
like a curtain.
—*Psalm 104: 1, 2*

SCRAPS

Lena Goldman Speaks of Sonya

Garment workers from Triangle always came to my cafe.
Each Saturday the boys and girls in groups, arm in arm
and laughing. You'd think after fourteen hours packing
and sewing they'd be ready to drop! But not on payday.

Sometimes Sonya sat alone, scribbling on scraps.
With such hours at Triangle, five brothers at home,
where else to write? Her poems weren't Moon-June or
like that. At first she only wanted us to laugh.

There was a cruel boss named Asch
who preferred his potatas mashed.
When the women talked union, he was thrashin
and stewin. Soft-in-the-head, Joseph Asch.

Oh, she was a bright one! Serious poems too:
Tonight all over the world
garment girls are looking out
looking up at stars...

Fourteen years old and writing English!
Well after the Fire, her father came in crying.
"Like losing her twice," he kept saying—
since Sonya's notebook burned up too.

He can't afford to educate his sons.
Yet even in better times, a daughter
wasn't sent to the House of Studies.
"But in America," Sonya said, "I will find my way."

FOUR FROM SONYA

Is the room swept, blankets
pressed and folded chairs
lined in readiness straight
oh hang the heavenly picture.

Writing poems with a cardboard
bookcase my only company
the poplar tree shifting shades
and whispering: remember me.

Boarding houses yes
lived in four or five or more.
Don't think I'll ever get
the smell of urine, frying
potatas and Evening in Paris
outa my head.

Going outside sunny sunny
rubbing leaves try to
out eclipse each other.

Did the notebook burn?

Stealing poetry?

DEAR UNCLE STANISLAUS

March 18, 1911

I pray this letter finds you in good health.
Coming over, a great storm. Water came down the ship
chimneys. Eight drowned. Thanks to Our Lady, I survive.

Uncle, do not believe gold lies in the street.
This is no golden land. Still I have work enough with
bread and meat to eat.

Such noise in this nation! All hours people shout.
Always factory bells and whistles. Up in the loft the
clatter of cloth in machines.

Uncle, write. Tell me, did the potatoes freeze
this Winter? If so, what was to eat? Could you sell
the wheat?

Next to Triangle Waist is a park with flowers and
birds. But who has time to enjoy? Who will pay for
that? Soon it will be Easter and at last a holiday.

They say with everyone coming here, Europe will soon
be empty. Next payday I am sending money. Give my love to
Auntie but save the large part for yourself.

Love,
Marie

P.S. Uncle, did our storks come back this Spring?

Speaking for the dead

CUTTER AND MOTHER

1.
Each morning children squeezed
inside a wire cage that pierced
the pit at extreme speed. SLAM.

At six, my mother went to the colliery
alongside her cousins and brothers.
Foremen liked them thin and short

For dynamiting narrow tunnels.
She recalls tall ones were trappers
waiting alone for the rolling-down

Black shaft and only a split-second
to jump aside, open-shut trap door.
She's proud none of her sons spend

Daylight crawling into darkness.
Not harnessed and roped like pit
ponies. No. Not one.

2.
Before first shaft of morning
I put bread and cheese in my sleeve,
walk down to Triangle Shirtwaist.

My knife cuts away from daylight,
carves layers round the paper patterns.
Sleeves, collars, flaps; white scraps

Fall to the floor. Pile up dove-tails,
wings, eight stories over the streets
and tunnels. But Mother what about

Parts deep inside me, what you can't
see with your eyes. For twelve hours
not a soft word spoken. Machines scream

For more cloth, faster, more cloth.
And at night, to fall exhausted into
dreams that bring no music or painted

Pictures. Mother even the pit pony
that is beaten gets a sweet to eat
pat on her head once in a while.

IMAGINING THE HORSE

Captain Meehan's horse, Yale,
was the first to arrive on the scene.

My name is Yale. At first
Hail of cinders.
Glass. Fire bells.
Falling bales and
timbers. Blood-smell.

Then:
Tarp-covered mounds.
Waterfalls from windows.
Hoses tangled in bundles.
Gutters red to fetlocks.

Night:
Searchlight.
Block and tackle.
Gray men in lines.
Stacks on wagons.

Journey:
Slow pull up Broadway
to Fourteenth to Fourth Avenue to
Twenty-third. Clanging. Wailing.
Twenty-sixth Street Pier.

Dawn:
The Sun has dropped
her mares and foals.
Plentiful as flies.
Wrapped in rows.

the horse speaks —
permission to write
a fragmented
narrative :)

TWENTY-SIXTH STREET PIER

A temporary morgue

1.
Half-past midnight, a hailstorm
broke, smashing in the roof glass.
Arc lights spun and sputtered,
rain and hail fell on faces in rows.
Policemen swung their lanterns low,
picked out the glass, copied down
numbers from the caskets.

night after the fire?

2.
I tell ya, folks here still
call the pier "Misery Lane."
Not so long ago you'd see
the blind and insane
beggars and homeless-old
boarding for the poorhouse
or the T.B. hospital.

Boats off to bedlam
or the penitentiary.
Landing them forever
on the islands
in the river.

3.
A double line of winos lifted
the bodies, followed the carts
to the Twenty-sixth Street Pier.

Mornings when the families came
panhandlers poured them coffee,
held up the fainting.

You can always get derelicts ✓
to do the dirty work.

4.
A derelict speaks *— a lot of direction*

Opium dives, canned-heat alleys
a night in the can's better than
coppers and corpses. I'd rather
the dry-heaves from dogcheap rotgut
or the DT's than seeing brothers
search for their sisters or
mothers calling their sons.

This says a whole hell of a lot

MERCER STREET PRECINCT REPORT

1.
One gent's watchcase
one man's garter
one razor strop.

One-half dozen postcards
one yellow metal ring
one one-dollar bill.

One lady's purse with rosary
one small mirror
one pin with painted picture.

2.
One pin with painted picture

Earthwork windmill rises, boxed arms
tilted to white heavens. Then little
wood sticks stalk garden walk.

Birds weaving cumulus dive to tulips
named for wishes: Yellow Moonstruck,
Windsor Castle, Tender Shepherd.

Inside shuttered cottage walls,
Kit and Kat lick whiskers, purr
by fire. Kettle spurts water.

list is interesting what does the 2nd stanza do?

THE FOLLOWING

Sure as smoke follows flame they came:
"Souvenirs from Triangle! Rosaries! Earrings!
Get your machinist's cap—or laces from his boots!
Hair ribbons from a dead girl's head!"

Sure as fish brings flies. Rabbi warned us
"Schnorrers"—solicitors for phony "funeral funds"—
would come when all along it was the Hebrew Free Burial
that was paying. "Sure as flood brings mud," he said.

A few from the Social Register ordered chauffeurs
to drive directly to police lines, demand they
be let through, so as to view this "spectacle."
Sure as carrion brings buzzards.

Ladies in lace shirtwaists, gentlemen in frock-coats
out for a Sunday stroll, filed up Fifth Avenue,
caught the stage-buses to the Twenty-sixth Street Pier.
High-hats in the long lines leading to the dead.

"I AM APPALLED"

New York Governor Dix

The Police Commissioner
gripes to the Mayor who points at
the Governor, "I am appalled,"
who sets on the State Labor Commissioner
who blames the National Fire Underwriters
who turn on the Fire Commissioner
who cites the "City Beautiful"
(for finding fire escapes ugly)
who then faults the Architects
who place it on Tenement Housing
who says failure of the Health Department
who then proclaim conspiracy
between the Utility Companies and
the Police Commissioner.

Love it!
The blame, the cycle,
the disregard, the
Speakers are men,
the dead are
women

I made sackcloth also my garment;
and I became a proverb to them.
—Psalm 69: 11

AT REST IN GREENWOOD

Jennie Franco

My short years wrap me like a cloth
of schooldays, feast days, my First Communion dress.
The cord of mornings, stitching at Triangle
up in the loft before light.

I trace the thread to my last, my fifteenth birthday.
Ribbons of friends dance the Tarantella,
circling plates of tortoni and ices
out on our stoop after dark.

And Mama says, don't forget Our Lady
and always light a holy candle on your birthday.
Today she twists rosary beads between my ruined fingers,
plaits roses in my veil.

Neighbors nail flowers, black crepe
to the doors, they have covered my face
with lilies and forget-me-nots.
I am circled with tapers.

I rest in the front room
next to the room where I was born.
The brass band wraps up our street,
"Panis Angelicus" stops at our stoop.

The Sons of Italy and Saint Angelo Society
have hired a cart just for my flowers.
Papa says, only the best for our Jennie.
A fine lady, I am lifted into my carriage.

The brass-harp of hymns follows the line
of Eleventh Street. Inside its woven voice
I know each murmuring Ave Maria.
The sky smells like lilies.

Slower. Silence. We are nearing Triangle.

Now the shock of the skeleton loft
unfolds the tall wall of wailing till
Heaven cracks and tatters, blesses us with rain.

FUNERAL FOR THE NAMELESS

Rose Schneiderman speaks

For miles the bereaved stream
under a single banner:
"We Demand Fire Protection."

The bunting's blue dye drips down
arms and faces of the honor guard,
eight of our youngest garment girls.

From the tops of tenements
bending out of windows
watching us.

Women, children, the old ones
lean on sashes, stare through
rain screen, down to deep street

Where white horses draped in black net
pull an empty hearse, mountain of blossoms.
As we march up Fifth Avenue

There they are on tops of hundreds of
buildings—structures no different from
the Asch Building and as for lacking

Fire protection, many much worse
than Triangle. It is this, not
cold rain, that makes me sick.

At each curb's turning, window-banks
empty of waving white handkerchiefs.
Thunder drums down the narrow stairways.

Thousands pour to Evergreen where over
the empty pits, rabbi, priest, preacher
bless the waiting coffins.

With holy water, hymns, their prayers
pronounce the placards' numerals:
46, 50, 61, 95, 103, 115, 127.

SURVIVOR'S CENTO

All through the day rain ever and again.
The quartet from the Elks Lodge sang "Abide with Me."
They lost both daughters, Sara and Sarafine.
Last year I was one of the pickets arrested and fined.
We were striking for open doors, better fire escapes.
Freda Velakowski, Ignatzia Bellota, Celia Eisenberg.
You knew the families from the flowers nailed to the doors.
That's my mama. Her name's Julia Rosen.
I know by her hair. I braid it every morning.
Now the same police who clubbed the strikers
keep the crowd from trampling on our bodies.
Sadie Nausbaum, Gussie Bierman, Anna Cohen, Israel Rosen.
I know that's my daughter, Sophie Salemi.
See that darn in her knee? Mended her stockings, yesterday.
Box one-twelve: female, black stockings, black shoes,
part of a skirt, a white petticoat, hair ribbons.
I would be a traitor to these poor burned bodies
if I came to talk good fellowship: Jennie Franco, Rose Weiner,
Julia Aberstein, Joseph Wilson, Nicolina Nicolese.
I found a mouse on the ninth floor, took it home,
kept it for a pet. At least it was still alive.
Our children go to work in firetraps, come home and sleep
in firetraps. Day and night they are condemned.
Ninth floor looked like a kindergarten. We were eight,
nine, ten. If the Inspector came, they hid us in bins.
Rose Feibush, Clotild Terdanova, Mary Leventhal.
That one's Catherine Maltese, and those, her daughters.
Lucia, she's twenty, Rosalie—she'd be fourteen.
Those two are sisters. Bettina and Frances Miale. M-I-A-L-E.
We asked the Red Cross worker how to help
and she said bring books—Tolstoy, Shakespeare in Yiddish.
Benny Costello said he knew his sister Della by her new shoes.
Anna Ardito, Gussie Rosenfield, Sara Kupla, Essie Bernstein,
reminders to spend my life fighting these conditions. Antonia
Colleti, Daisy Lopez Fitze, Surka Brenman, Margaret Schwartz.
One coffin read: Becky Kessler, call for tomorrow.
The eighth casket had neither name nor number. It contained
fragments from the Fire, picked up but never claimed.

Cento is a Latin word for a garment made of patches.

JURY OF PEERS

Morris Baum, sales.
Leo Abraham, real estate.
Abraham Akerstrom, clerk.
Arlington Boyce, management.
H. Houston Hierst, importer.
Harry Roeder, painter.
William Ryan, sales.
Victor Steinman, shirts.
Anton Scheuerman, cigars.
Charles Vetter, buyer.

Mister Hierst summarized:
I've listened to the witnesses
and my conscience is clear.
Harris and Blanck are pretty
good managers. We've reached
the decision that the type
of girl you have at Triangle
is basically less intelligent.
Hell, excuse me, Your Honor,

judgment

But most of em can't even read
or speak English—and the way
they live! They're lots
less intelligent than the
type of female you find
in other walks of life. I mean
that kinda worker is more—
well—susceptible to panic.
Emotional females can't

Keep a clear head they
panicked and jumped my
conscience is clearly
Act of Almighty
God they jumped
conclusion Your
Honor owners
of Triangle
not guilty.

fragments closing in

The children which thou shalt have
after thou hast lost the others
shall say again in thy ears:
The place is too strait for me;
give place to me that
I may dwell.
—*Isaiah 49: 20*

GRAND STREET

After Sophie Ruskay

We lined the walks in chalk boxes, numbers.
Played potsy with markers of tin. Or spinning
tops, we'd only stop for the hokeypokey man who
sold a slap of ice cream on a piece of paper for
a penny. Papa complained potsy and dancing wore
shoe soles through in just two weeks and told us
not to leave our block. Still I skipped to

Grand Street to dream at the dolls in windows.
Each splendid in real silk and lace. Blue eyes,
golden hair. Their brass-bound trunks for travel
brimmed kidskin boots and fur-trimmed bonnets.
One mamselle in ashes-of-roses held a pink parasol.
At her feet, a white batiste shirtwaist was displayed.
The kind Mama made at Triangle. Back before the Fire.

WHITE LIGHT

After Sonya Levien

It's not easy to teach us union.
Garment girls shift like sand, start
too young in the trade, wait for

Prince Charming to take em away.
When I arrived from Russia
my cheeks like apples. And look now!

But talk about a dreaming fool!
Me, thirteen in the Golden Land
longing to work at Life and Love.

Be what you call a builder of bridges.
Yes, I'd go back, show all Moscow
a great American lady.

My first position: feeding kerchiefs
to machine. First English sentence:
"Watch your needle—three thousand stitches

A minute." Say, I was some swift kid
in those days: seventy-two hundred
an hour, eighty-six thousand pieces

A day, four dollars in the pay
envelope—and that the busy season.
for three months my pay was bread.

I yearned to earn wages, save my
little sister's passage, I was so
lonely in America. Soon like the rest

I grieved at my machine, swore I'd
marry any old man just to get out.
One by one the others left to marry

But returned to Triangle. In them
I saw my future in a white heat light
no dreams could soften.

SHIRTWAIST TUCKER

After Sadie Hershy

The Fire? That was
Nineteen-and-eleven.
Yes I was a garment girl
a tucker at Triangle.
We'd haul big bolts of cloth
feed em to pleating machines
that crimped the folds
at neck and wrists—
to take in fullness or
decorate the yoke.
Saturday was payday—
twelve dollars for sixty hours!
Oh I could make do
better than most though
Winter was bitter
and prices dear.
Bit by bit bought me
a warm wool coat.
And in Spring
a white batiste waist.
Was a real American lady
come High Holy Days!
Say that was a slave-driving place.
Couldn't talk to your neighbors
and the bosses kept doors locked.
Looking out for organizers.
Agitators.
That afternoon I was close by
the cutting-table
spied a little snake of smoke.
So I says to the manager
"Mr. Bernstein I see smoke."
And when he tipped water from
a little wooden bucket
such a flame shot up!

POTTER'S FIELD

After Thomas Horton

A few of us back then were porters in the district
bundling scraps under the cutting-table or
after the packers crated the shirtwaists—why,
we'd haul them on down to Washington Place.
My grammaw told me when she was a girl
Washington Park was a potter's field and used
to say the nameless passed to glory anyway.
Soon as the high-class built here, potter's field
became a park with bushes and benches,
a garden spot for their fancy townhouses.
(We laughed at how those homeless bones
were pushing up a monument to President Washington
who once sold a slave for a bolt of cotton cloth.)
Then the factories came and company housing—
tenements you call em. Crowded! You don't know
the word! But you want to hear about the Fire.

Well, Giuseppe had fainted so I ran the car with Gaspar.
When the fire broke out and the elevator broke down
I kept the machine from smashing in the basement.
'Cause of the smoke we couldn't see the floors
had to open up the doors by guesswork.
Girl, I ran that car till it couldn't run no more,
why we were puttin in switch cables
till they ran with water and stuck.
Circuit breakers were blowing out all over the place.
The ladies were jumping on my car, even slid down
the ropes—why there were twenty on the roof!
The ones that got inside grabbed at Gaspar's arms,
pulled his hair, jabbed his face. Christ A-mighty!
They were climbin on the cables!
That was the passenger car, you understand.
Later I read in the *Tribune* a big iron bar locked
the freight elevators—no, never could use em.
I'm the only Negro to testify at the trial.
The headlines named me "Heroic Elevator Man."

STITCHER

For Judith Hall

It was soon after the Fire
I was employed as a housemaid.
Now I wash the garments and
some I starch. Stiff as grief

Or courage. That flat iron presses
and gives shine. In the morning
there are lamps to fill, globes
wiped so light can shine through.

Windows thrown open for sweeping
and dusting. Mid-days, Mistress
sometimes recites scriptures or
legends like Paramhansa the swan

Who could sup up milk, leave
water in the saucer. She says we
separate pure from impure in our
breathing, that new cells replace

The old. I know remade garments
bring fair material from that
judged hopeless and so my needle
joins torn places, mends worn parts.

[handwritten note: a lot of this is about mending / fragments from the fire]

Each stitch carries a blessing.
Don't you know handkerchiefs keep
secrets, that hat trims see hair
as a halo of the spirit, crown of Life?

A skillful housemaid will not pour
boiling water over flannel or use
strong soap on silk or organdy.

In the evenings, I've learned
the Language—alphabet, vocabulary,
grammar rote by gaslight sputter.

[handwritten note: who is she speaking to?]

Tonight I write this history
into my copy book: Gehenna.
Gehenna, a word for garbage burning

Outside the walls of Jerusalem.
The refuse of the city. Corpses
of criminals, sacrificed animals.

Holocaust of relics, regrets, evil
memories released into smoke.

SACRISTAN

Before Mass, I fill silver cruets
with wine, water, place pressed linen
under pallboard, over chalice, lavabo.
The priest's vestments must be laid
just so—blue for Lady Day, purple
during Lent, white for first-class
feasts, green for ordinary, always

Red to commemorate the death
-dates of the martyrs. We study
the lives of Lawrence and St. Joan
and in a symbol book look up
their signs of stake and gridiron.
When the sanctuary lamp burns low
I'll trim the wick and fill the oil,

Trade candelabra stubs for tall,
taking care to pare beeswax drips
from the tops of golden holders.
Fresh charcoal, sandalwood incense
for the censor. And now to work
before the morning bell! Rags,
brushes, mops. Scrub and shine

Steps, pews, floor. Ora Labora.
Labora Ora. Prayer is labor,
labor the prayer. I polish and
pray the names of my brother,
of all the shirtwaist martyrs,
so these holy ones may intercede
for us on earth.

In my monastic breviary I mark
any mention of fire or garments
and collect those psalms into
my copy book. I've composed
a homily on the example
of the beekeeper who handles
her charges, yet is not stung.

NINTH FLOOR REPRISE

Fifty-eight girls crowded into a cloakroom.

The glass blackens and shatters.
Who will come for us?

Up on Tenth, typists and bookkeepers leave
ledgers to ashes, machines to melt.
The packers and switchboard-lady gone
the phone cords and crate slats spurt
split into stars and meteors.

Up on Tenth, our finished shirtwaists unfold,
crack the crates, jump upright, join sleeves,
dance the hora and mazurka, spin like dreidels.
They call to us, their makers:
Stitcher, Presser, Cutter, Tucker.

"I saw them piled," testified Fireman Wohl,
"they pressed their faces toward a little window."

Gather up the fragments that
remain, that nothing be lost.
—*John 6: 12*

STADIUM SESTINA

Remembering high school commencement
while researching the Triangle Fire of March 25, 1911

The poorest student—me—with the loudest voice reads the
       script:
"Mother of Exiles from her beacon-hand. . . ."
Our town in the stadium bleachers looks down on circumstance.
In the east, the Triangle papers slowly rise on imperfect wings
of file folders, pamphlets, fly to this valley of newsprint
song sheets. Where are the words of fire for my generation?

Our parents and teachers became the first generation
after that of 1911, the year these martyrs taught History the
       script.
Their shredded alphabets of flames pierced the clouds of
       newsprint.
(Ashes are drifting seventy years to light on my left writer's hand.)
At Commencement, our graduation sleeves split in wings,
the orchestra strikes up Pomp and Circumstance.

The owners of Triangle profited from fires (all were created
       circumstance).
From Europe, Italy, Jamaica, Palestine, Russia—the immigrant
       generation
crossed to Ellis Island, bundles piled, shawls spread in wings.
Each wage-earner signed an "X" or Arabic-Cyrillic-Hebrew script.
On payday, March 25, 1911, no one knew how many were
       on hand—
the hired and fired, dispensable as newsprint.

The *Herald, Sun, Telegraph*, and *Times* set photos into
       newsprint,
hurried to interview witnesses, each tried to scoop the
       circumstance.

...Now Commencement ends. The principal shakes my hand,
pronounces: "We pass the torch to a new generation."
Every year the same old line ends the script.
Whether graduation or when our town's a tour-stop for the Wings

Over Jordan Choir—black angels singing God's chillen got
    shoes/ harps/ wings.
Since the time of Triangle, turpentine torches of rags and
    newsprint
were replaced by gas lamps, then by electric arc lights. So says
    the *Script*
for the Centennial. Citizens in beards and bonnets recreated the
    circumstance
and Miss Liberty raised her beacon flashlight beside golden
    generations
of post-Depression years. (Few thought McCarthyism had gotten
    out of hand.)

The pageant showed the founding of our town and how folks lived
    hand-to-hand
until Henry Ford and the Great War opened Prosperity's
    war-bond-wings
over Union Carbide and the First National Bank. But the
    pilgrim generation
inside Triangle bent their backs, stitched at flimsy thinner than
    newsprint.
The scrap piles, oil pans, and wicker baskets their circumstance.
Families followed the multiple hearses. One father held a
    pasteboard script

In his hand: "This is the funeral of Yetta Goldstein." He follows
    the newsprint
march-map under clouds split in wings. "Heavens Wept"
    headlines the circumstance.
All this before Commencement or my generation—back when
    flames wrote the script.

TRIANGLE SITE

Asch Building, 1911; Brown Building, 1981

Soaked to skin, look through lens
at Eighth, Ninth, Tenth. So this
is where they worked, I thought

How hot the loft on summer days
and say aloud the layers learned
from photogravure fashion plates:

Pantaloons, petticoats, hour-glass
corsets, one cover called a camisole.
So many strings! In the spinning

Mills down South, steam looms boomed
and even in Winter children stripped
to their shifts, baby hands slick

On cotton bobbins. The shutter clicks,
a pigeon struts and springs. So this
is where they fell. Or jumped.

Layers billow, catch broken rails,
like sails slap on light posts or
pile high on iron fence spears

Where like a little boat, one
pierced shoe holds a paper rose
stem up.

SEAR

July 1982

Always adding. Revising this manuscript.
I plant *direct quotations* on the page,
arranging line-breaks, versification.

Newspaper files: Frances Perkins speaks
from the street, *I felt I must sear it*
not only on my mind but on my heart
forever. One mother, *When will it be*
safe to earn our bread? Their words.
Yet some call that schmaltz, soap-opera-

Sentiment, Victorian melodrama. Riding
the subway, smoke fizzes in my ears and
in my room, electric heater coils glow
*C*s and *O*s in the box. To write about *them*
yet not interfere, although I'm told
a poet's task is to create a little world.

A testimony: Two tried to stay together
on the ledge, but suddenly one twisted
and plunged, a burning bundle. The other
looked ahead, arms straight out, speaking
and shouting *as if addressing an invisible*
audience. She gestured an embrace then

Jumped. Her name was Celia
Weintraub. She lived
on Henry Street.

THE DAY WHEN MOUNTAINS MOVED

The mountain-moving day is coming.
I say so, yet others doubt.
Only awhile a mountain sleeps.
In the past
All mountains moved in fire
Yet you may not believe it.
Oh man, this alone believe
All sleeping women now will
awake and move.

—*Yosano Akiko, 1911*

SOURCES

Akiko, Yosano. "The Mountain Moving Day." *Japan Quarterly,*
     Tokyo International, San Francisco, April-June 1984.
Elson, Hilbert. "Improved Labor Laws Result from Triangle Fire
     Fifty Years Ago." *Industrial Bulletin* . New York State Dept.
     of Labor, Albany, New York, March 1961.
Howe, Irving, and Kenneth Libo. *How We Lived: A Documentary
     History of Jews in America 1880-1930.* Richard Marek Publish-
     ers, Inc., New York, 1979.
Kuniczak, W. S. *My Name Is Million: An Illustrated History of the
     Poles in America.* Doubleday & Company, Inc., New York, 1978.
Militz, Annie. *Spiritual Housekeeping.* Master-Mind Press, Los
     Angeles, 1925.
O'Sullivan, Judith, and Rosemary Gallick. *Workers and Allies: Female
     Participation in the American Trade Union Movement 1824-
     1976.* Smithsonian Instutution Traveling Exhibition Service,
     Washington, D. C., 1975.
Saperstein, Saundra. "Reliving Pain." *The Washington Post*, February
     1, 1979.
Schneiderman, Rose, and Lucy Goldwaithe. "Triangle Memorial Service."
     In *All for One.* Paul S. Ericksson, Inc., Middlebury, Vermont,
     1967.
Stein, Leon, ed. *Out of the Sweatshop.* Fitzhenry and Whiteside, Ltd.,
     Toronto, 1977.
Stein, Leon. *The Triangle Fire.* J. B. Lippincott Company,
     Philadelphia, 1962.
Wertheimer, Barbara. *We Were There.* Pantheon Books, a division of
     Random House, Inc., New York, 1977.

ILLUSTRATIONS:

1. HESTER STREET (Courtesy of the Library of Congress)
2. SIDEWALK DEAD (Courtesy of Brown Brothers)
3. TRADE UNION PROCESSION FOR FIRE VICTIMS
       (Courtesy of the Library of Congress)
4. SHIRTWAIST STRIKERS (Courtesy of the Library of Congress)
5. GARMENT GIRLS, JUNE 1911 (Courtesy of Mrs.
       Florence Leebov, Pittsburgh)
6. LIPSHITZ & EISENBERG (Courtesy of the Library of Congress)

CREDITS

The author and publisher would like to thank these publications for premission to reprint the following poems:

STEAM DUMMY

"Grampa Thomas," *West Hills Review* ; "The Naphtha," *The Nation* ; "Drycleaners," Greater Flint Arts Council (an earlier version was published in *Larry's Poetry Review*); "Perches" *Working Cultures* ; From "Office for the Dead"—"Fleeth as it were a shadow" as "Carbon Copies" in *Talkin' Union* No. 2, "Of whom shall we seek for succour" as "Daydream" in *Quest : A Feminist Quarterly* ;"Blessed are they who die in the Lord" as "In Memoriam: Carolyn Johnson" in *Calling Home: Working-Class Women's Writings* ; "We shall not all sleep but we shall all be changed" as "Two A.M. Moving Day" in *West Hills Review*— "Portrait of a Packer," *Ploughshares;* "Biology I," *The Cooke Book: A Seasoning of Poets* (Scop Publications); "Eavesdropping," *The Columbus Dispatch*; "Preparation for Decoration Day" *st. helena*, "Euthanasia," *Warren Wilson Review*; "Windows," *West Hills Review* ; "Sheaves" *Pudding Magazine;* "Great Oaks Home Poem," *The Heartlands Today III*

FRAGMENTS FROM THE FIRE

"The Great Divide," and "Ninth Floor Reprise" in *Building Blocks*, National Center for Urban Ethnic Affairs; "March 25, 1911" in *The Washington Review*; "Twenty-sixth Street Pier," "At Rest in Greenwood" and "Potter's Field" in *Quindaro*; "Funeral for the Nameless" in *The Chester H. Jones Foundation National Poetry Competition Winners 1983*; "White Light" in *Talkin' Union*; "Stitcher" in *13th Moon*; "Sear" in *Evidence of Community*, Center for Wasington Area Studies; and "Triangle Site," in *Working Culture*.

Photographs on pages 88, 102, 107, 110, 121 courtesy of the Library of Congress.
Photograph on page 95 is courtesy of Brown Brothers.
Photograph on page 75 is courtesy of Florence Leebov.

Cover Photos: "Porter's Drycleaning plant, 1927" courtesy of Elizabeth Poeter; "Garment Workers, Pittsburgh, 1911" courtesy of Florence Leebov.